Rolleen Rabbit's Book of Short Poems

Rowena Kong

Annie Ho

ROLLEEN RABBIT

"Just look closer and you could see the meaning of infinity in the simplest of things…"

First Printing: 2022

ISBN: 978-1-990782-46-6

Dedicated to the sick and hurt bunnies of Jericho Beach, Vancouver, whose courage and resilience for survival paints a story of hope and determination for a challenging future.

SPRING DAWN

The season finally changes as the colours return,

gracing the land with splendid hues of pinks and reds.

Sweet buds flourishing under the rising spring glow;

chirpy young birds flap their wings and alight on tender branchlets.

The plum blossoms have arrived to sing of the golden dawn anew;

another beginning to cherish from heaven its youthful dew.

A Father's Pride

The praises from a father are like the glow of moonlight on a darker night.

They cast favour on his anticipating child from amongst the crowds.

The child looks upward to them like the towering sky above.

They give him a countenance of hope and confidence to last throughout his journey.

The Heart of a Mother and Father

How a mother and father cherish their child;

Will they be cherished by their child in return?

The scolding from a father and mother may be repetitive,

like the constant dripping of raindrops.

Nonetheless, they are more precious and costly than golden silence.

A Great Company

How fulfilling it is to scale the mountain heights with one's father;

And times more endearing when sipping rose tea with one's mother.

As we hike, the song of the forest birds turns melodious;

The rush of waters dance in tandem.

Roses were never this fragrant and sweet as we converse 'till midnight.

Fleeting Flattery

Flattery and exaggerated expressions; they are but a flicker in a full day's light.

They shine unsteadily before vanishing into thin air.

They charm but never taught a lesson.

Yet, one longs to hear them; they are a source of arousal.

When truth comes contradictory, all their worth is lost.

They are better unsaid; worse than unheard in the first place.

Therefore, keep those words few and utter only where necessary.

Because you might end up a thousand times more hurt than before.

And lie searching for that word of comfort to dispel the fragrance of flattery.

Two Mirrors

I brought two jars with me to the well,

One a little larger, the other a little smaller,

The moon lit up the expanse of the night heavens.

I scoop and drew water, filling each jar to the brim.

I looked down at both jars on my fraternal twins.

They were as fair as the moon, but with stillness so vulnerable.

I smiled and they grinned.

One a little plump, the other a little slim.

We were like a family; I wish we would never part.

Mindfulness Night

Amidst the silent nurturing in the dark,

The seeds germinate.

Thus, in the stillness of a moonlit night,

Thoughts and reminiscence flourish.

The evening air and breeze sweep over the place,

Like restful peace descending and enveloping the earth.

My mind, both unperturbed and energetic,

Plays with the winds of inspiration and taps to the beat of nightfall nature.

Always, Twelve Months of Blossoms

The first month's snow and cold,

Mark the purity of a year's beginning.

Yet, out bursts dainty snowdrops gracing the icy white ground.

So pure and tender, like a new birth springing into life.

The second month's chills and flurries,

Precede winter's finale and promise transition,

Primroses gather in colorful arrays,

Reviving one's love and pleasure for the sentimental.

The third month's rays and breezes,

Welcome a revival of gradual blooms and sprouting leaves.

Plum blossoms of pinks, whites and reds are budding richly.

They tell of Eastern stories to the young and old.

The fourth month's sounds and sweetness,

Echo a new cycle of abundant life and goodness.

Seas of cherry blossoms paint an artful of landscape.

They return to bask the city in beauty and grace.

The fifth month's warmth and chatter,

Invite all to cherish and celebrate.

Tulip fields of all colours and shapes,

Charm sightseers and nature lovers to the brim.

The sixth month's feasts and drinks,

Call for enjoyment of mid-year's fanfare.

Cheerful pansy flowers add pleasure for the crowds.

They smile for nature's gratitude and delight.

The seventh month's heat and sweat,

Heighten energy for leisure and engagements.

Roses come to light up and redraw the garden.

They send new greetings of love and fragrance to an expectant world.

The eighth month's endurance and strength,

Reaffirm our love for the shores and skies.

Sunflowers grant us a splash of golden browns and yellows.

The brightness of their faces radiates bold sturdiness and joy.

The ninth month's gusts and foliage,

Reverberate another season's blow.

Purple asters entice new throngs of bees to pollinate.

They stand steadfast and hardy against the winds.

The tenth month's harvest and festivities,

Share thoughts and resolutions for everyone's undertakings.

Japanese Anemones flourish their pinks and oranges.

Petals of five, round and soft, graciously mesmerise.

The eleventh month's draughts and downpours,

Herald the impending winter of year-end.

Clusters of light pinkish stonecrop line and fill our garden edges.

They make a perfect colour match for the red roofed patio.

The twelfth month's frost and sniffles,

Mark the rest of a year's ending.

Poinsettia reds linger close with the greens of Christmas hollies,

Colouring a celebration that has lasted over a thousand years.

Gracious Wisdom

Better is the wise man who thinks he is not wise,

Than a naysayer who thinks he knows every fault of another.

Streams of clarity fill the minds of the wise,

Like a lasting and uninhibited flow that never runs dry.

The mountains stand in witness of wise judgement and structure.

They cast benevolent glances on people of conscience.

For conscience guides the steps of the prudent.

A compassionate offering, they will not dismiss.

Wisdom is a gracious teacher who finds the good in every broken pieces.

A Winding Life

Like the winding course of river meanders through mountain valleys,

So is the journey down one's paths in life.

They bend and encircle, hardly a straight channel throughout.

Standing and staring at the same level with the river meandering,

One may not see as far, for it winds back and forth,

Without a flicker of the end in sight.

Behind you and before you, the waters look the same,

Making no progress and endlessly frustrate.

Not until, one could see from above.

Oh, what beauty is such to behold,

The divinely crafted wonder and winding channels of the river meandering so strong,

Bold enough to cut through challenges of low plains and high valleys combined.

Board Game at the Beach

At the summer beach where the children play,

To picnic tables, we also brought our board game to play.

The light clicking of many tokens on our board could not be compared,

With the squeals and screams of those fun-loving children.

With each move across our board,

A little girl shouts and giggles.

With each winning gain,

A toddler tossing his ball yells and screeches.

With each loss and capture,

A lad hurls his best throw and cheers on.

With the progress of our game at its height, we patiently press on,

Until a loud splatter of a seagull's droppings on our board they unexpectedly fall.

A Not So Silent Match

Once, we started our chess game,

I placed my blacks, and you arranged your whites.

The gushing stream waters flowed along.

Gaze affixed; a pair of fox sparrows sang.

Our thoughts to each divided, we planned in deliberation.

The clock struck past noon; silence once more interrupted.

You sighed and threw in the towel,

"A hastened move," you said.

I smiled and advanced another knight.

The second hand ticked by under the rays.

A round face, a square face,

The shape of a clock made no difference.

Just a few more positioning and moves,

Who would gain and who would lose?

The Feel of Spring

Down the cherry blossom lane, I strolled.

Blanketing soft pinks, reds and whites spread all across,

Sheltering emerald green grass away from sight.

Bending over, they smell crisp and pure,

Showering sweetness as a plump chickadee comes to revere.

The sky helps paint an expanse of blue,

Matching the petals' hues at the peak of their bloom.

Gazing upwards, the morning sun casts a radiant glow.

The kind flowers gently reflect the light.

The brightening of the petals follows.

The blossoms form a protective canopy overhead,

That watches one steadily with outstretched branches.

The brown gray chickadee lands and pecks enthusiastically,

Indifferent to a keen observer.

It cherishes every moment of its play with the tender soft petals,

As if unwilling to part with another beauty like itself.

They are a second pair of perfect match,

Like a symphony in harmony one could not bear to forget.

Longing for Spring

Diverse colours of foliage are to autumn,

As charming cherry blossoms are to spring.

Here, under the sounds of autumn rain,

Churns yearnful nostalgia for the dawn of spring petals.

Chilly forceful winds are to autumn,

As soothing colours of bloom are to spring.

Here, under the rising cold of autumn weather,

Drives the melodious tune for the welcoming of next spring.

Nature's Symphony

Quenching the darkness, the dawn emerges.

How perfect is the eternal trails of the sun.

Morning is revived and showers light upon all.

Gracious dewdrops found their rest on loving petals.

Five little ducklings follow the lead of their mother.

Upon the lake waters they stay faithful in company.

She quacks and they listen.

Her presence is their steadfast assurance.

The various sights and sounds of nature speak of care divine.

They move and reverberate,

Playing symphony with time.

Against such, there is no peace.

Notes so pure and breeze so soft;

Stories both told and untold;

They complement each other like ripples through the water.

Seven musical notes and seven rainbow colours; they prevail in harmony forever.

Rain Command

Beads after beads; raindrops keep falling and landing;

Splitting and merging all over my glass window.

Their fate is certainly lasting.

One leaves and another comes down again.

I gaze and wonder,

as each of them wanders like transparent armies under a central command.

The rain gives its orders, and they descend,

Like faithful troops from heaven.

My windows and walls became their territory gained.

Blossoms Through Time

How precious are the pretty forget-me-nots in

September,

And the cheerful dandelions in October.

Flowers first blooming in spring,

That last through autumn,

Are like soothing words uttered amid hurt.

Through the gardens of time,

words are like flowers,

and their nurture like evergreen leaves.

Their presence and sight speak volumes.

The gates of the gardens,

are our hearts through the seasons,

Where words seek to flow in and out.

Autumn is in need of spring,

Just as winter longs for summer.

For hope is both a longing and a certainty,

in a garden which never lack words to colour and fill.

EAST AND WEST

Morning and evening,

as moonlight in the East and sunbeams in the West;

as blossom trees flourish in the East and rose petals spread out in the West;

each kind of both exudes an abundance of fragrance to please their people.

From the land of the rising sun to the place of the setting sun,

as spring dawns and summer shines,

it is one wide expanse of an earth to treasure and cherish through time.

The Eternal Touch

Water freezes and snow falls.

Stone may break and crushed into pieces to drain.

Can pine withstand the lightning and force of hurricanes?

Bamboo is strong but hides the sun.

The moonlight is bright, but its reflected source that of the mighty sun.

Nonetheless, I hold eternity within the humble blossom petals on my well-

soothed palms,

for they are gentle and quiet spoken in heart,

and gracious enough to fully beautify my paths.

Complements

Flowers have butterflies and sky has clouds,

so water has rivers and sand has the shore.

Will words exceed space,

    or colours overflow the canvas?

Memories and eternity,

    will each surpass the other?

"Hope you have enjoyed our poems! Rolleen wishes you a nice day

ahead!"

Spring comes and
spring goes,
Like the sun, it is
coming back again.
A circuit so strong
and undefeatable,
It rises and de-
scends, like the tail
of the wind,
We meet and greet
thee, O Glory of the
seasons,

Resurrecting life and warmth to please humanity.
Please stay and tarry 'till we are forever satisfied,
To run the marathon of cheer and delight,
Fulfilling our devotion and steadfastness,
Through perpetual days with enduring moments
that colour and uphold our favours and
abounding grace!